THE CAMPER'S SURVIVAL GUIDE

THE
CAMPER'S
SURVIVAL
GUIDE

Food Prepping, Gear, First Aid,
Etiquette, and More!

Tamsin King

Racehorse Publishing

First Published by Summersdale Publishers Ltd, an imprint of Hachette UK, 2018.

First Racehorse Publishing edition, 2019.

Text by Sophie Martin.

Racehorse Publishing books may be purchased in bulk at special discounts for sales promotion, corporate gifts, fund-raising, or educational purposes. Special editions can also be created to specifications. For details, contact the Special Sales Department, Skyhorse Publishing, 307 West 36th Street, 11th Floor, New York, NY 10018 or info@skyhorsepublishing.com.

Racehorse Publishing™ is a pending trademark of Skyhorse Publishing, Inc.®, a Delaware corporation.

Visit our website at www.skyhorsepublishing.com.

10 9 8 7 6 5 4 3 2

Library of Congress Cataloging-in-Publication Data is available on file.

ISBN: 978-1-63158-409-1
E-Book ISBN: 978-1-63158-417-6

Printed in China

CONTENTS

BEFORE YOU GO

WHETHER YOU'RE NEW TO CAMPING OR YOU'VE DONE IT BEFORE, EACH TRIP CAN PRODUCE SURPRISES. IN THIS SECTION YOU'LL FIND TOP TIPS ON HOW TO PLAN FOR YOUR CAMPING TRIP, FROM DECIDING WHERE TO GO TO CHOOSING WHAT EQUIPMENT TO BUY AND WHICH CLOTHES TO TAKE WITH YOU.

DIFFERENT TYPES OF CAMPING

Traditional camping involved the sky above, the grass below, and the trees in front of the intrepid explorer who rocked up at their secluded spot with the bare minimum of equipment to see them through to the morning. But as camping has become more and more popular, thankfully it can cater not just to the intrepid explorer but the cautious vacationer—and anyone in between. Whether you want your camping trip to be a glamorous affair or as gritty as the soil beneath your feet, you can tailor your experience to suit your needs. Here are just some of the different types of camping to try out:

≈ CAMPGROUND CAMPING ≈

Campgrounds are the perfect venues for families or couples who are equipped with either a tent or a camper. You can even take your furry friend as a lot of sites are dog-friendly! Many campgrounds may refuse to cater to large groups of friends, and bachelor and bachelorette parties, so always check with the campground before you book. Basic campgrounds comprise a section of land to pitch up on, and usually provide shower and toilet facilities. Swankier campgrounds also provide entertainment areas, restaurants, bars, and childcare.

～ FESTIVAL CAMPING ～

Many people's first experience of camping is at a mainstream festival, where the atmosphere is constantly buzzing and the noise never dies down. This type of camping is very different from others, so don't be put off from camping altogether if you didn't enjoy it. If a big festival seems a bit daunting but you like the idea of attending something similar, there are tons of smaller-scale festivals that provide a lot more privacy—some even cater specifically to families.

≋ GLAMPING ≋

If you're a newbie to camping, why not start off with glamping, as it's a great way of being at one with nature while being guaranteed a comfortable night's sleep in a proper bed? Glamping accommodation comes in all forms: yurts, tepees, safari tents, and treehouses, to name a few. These are typically popular for groups of bachelors or bachelorettes, but also perfect for families and couples that are looking to escape from it all without having to buy all the camping equipment or worry about where to go to the bathroom.

～ WILD CAMPING ～

Essentially, wild camping is camping wherever you please in the countryside. However, every country has its own rules and regulations, so you must check them out before you set off, as you could be penalized otherwise. Here is a list of some countries and their wild camping laws:

★ **United States**—Wild, or backcountry, camping is allowed in most United States national parks. However, each park has different rules and regulations for those who want to escape the regulated campground experience. Visit the website for the National Park Service (www.nps.gov) for rules for specific parks around the country, as well as additional camping tips and suggestions.

★ **England, Northern Ireland, and Wales**— though most landowners tolerate respectful wild campers, wild camping without permission from the landowner is not allowed in any region apart from the Dartmoor National Park.

★ **Scotland**—wild camping is legal but there are guidelines that must be adhered to. Put simply, you must ensure that you're safe and respectful, and that you leave the spot exactly as you found it. Find out more at www.visitscotland.com/accommodation/ camper-camping/wild-camping.

★ **France**—the wild camping rules aren't hugely clear, although it's understood that with the landowner's permission it is generally accepted. However, lighting fires isn't allowed and you must set off before 9 a.m. the next day.

★ **Greece**—wild camping is illegal here.

★ **Norway and Sweden**—based on *allemannsretten* (the right to roam), these countries allow ramblers free rein to open country, and wild camping is encouraged as long as you're approximately 164 yards away from the nearest building and stay no longer than two nights if you don't have permission from the landowner. For more information, visit www.visitnorway.com/plan-your-trip/travel-tips-a-z/right-of-access.

WILD CAMPING ETIQUETTE

Assuming that your chosen country allows wild camping, here are some general rules to follow to ensure your respectfulness and safety during your stay:

★ Tell someone where you are going and for how long.

★ Be prepared for all weather conditions and eventualities.

★ Check for "no camping" signs before you pitch your tent.

★ Arrive late and leave early—wild camping is intended for sleeping at night only.

★ Make yourself as inconspicuous as possible.

★ Be considerate of your surroundings—this includes nature, animals, and people. If asked to move on, do so speedily and politely.

★ Check there are no water sources nearby then make your toilet hole approximately 6 inches deep in the earth. Cover up the hole and take your toilet paper with you when you go.

★ Start a fire only if safe to do so and monitor it at all times. Never light an open fire as it could be a danger to yourself and your environment. On leaving, ensure that the fire is completely extinguished.

★ Make sure the camping spot looks exactly the same when you leave as when you found it. *Never leave trash!*

THE OUTSIDE IS THE ONLY **PLACE WE CAN TRULY** BE INSIDE THE WORLD.

★ *Daniel J. Rice* ★

THE BEST COASTAL CAMPING SPOTS IN THE UNITED STATES

★ Cape Cod National Seashore, Massachusetts

★ Assateague Island, Assateague State Park, Maryland

★ Islamorada, Florida Keys, Florida

★ Wai'anapanapa State Park, Maui, Hawaii

★ Black Sand Beach, Alaska

★ Flamenco Beach, Puerto Rico

★ Little Tybee Island, Georgia

★ Cape Lookout National Seashore, North Carolina

★ Wright's Beach, Sonoma Coast State Park, California

★ Second Beach Trail, Olympic National Park, Washington

THE BEST COASTAL CAMPING SPOTS IN THE UK AND EUROPE

★ Calgary Beach, Isle of Mull, Scotland

★ Treen, West Cornwall

★ Aberafon, Llŷn Peninsula, North Wales

★ Clachtoll Beach, Lochinver, Sutherland

★ The Gower, South Wales

★ Ladram Bay, Devon

★ Morecambe Bay, Lancashire

★ Castlerock, Northern Ireland

★ Falsterbo, Skåne, Sweden

★ Chia, Sardinia, Italy

THE BEST COUNTRYSIDE CAMPING SPOTS IN THE UNITED STATES

- ★ Big Bend National Park, Texas

- ★ Glacier National Park, Montana

- ★ Carlsbad Caverns National Park, New Mexico

- ★ Denali National Park, Alaska

- ★ Pisgah National Forest, North Carolina

- ★ Shenandoah National Park, Virginia

- ★ Sequoia and Kings Canyon National Parks, California

- ★ Yellowstone National Park, USA

- ★ Grand Teton National Park, Wyoming

- ★ Great Smoky Mountains National Park, Tennessee

THE BEST COUNTRYSIDE CAMPING SPOTS IN THE UK AND EUROPE

★ Loch Lomond and the Trossachs, Scotland

★ Lake District National Park, Cumbria

★ The Black Mountains, Brecon Beacons, South Wales

★ Carneddau, Snowdonia, North Wales

★ Ugborough Moor, Dartmoor

★ The Cheviots, Borderlands, Northumberland

★ The Cairngorms, Scotland

★ La Fouly, The Alps, France

★ Hossa National Park, Finland

★ Connemara, Ireland

A GREAT MANY PEOPLE, *and more all the time,* **LIVE THEIR ENTIRE LIVES WITHOUT EVER ONCE SLEEPING OUT UNDER THE STARS.**

★ *Alan S. Kesselheim* ★

ORGANIZING THE PERFECT TRIP

There are so many locations in the world to travel to, and for some, the world is their oyster. If the idea of packing lightly, hopping on a plane, renting a car, and venturing to a remote location sounds perfect and you have the budget to make it happen, your camping adventure awaits; it might require more planning than other vacations but it'll be well worth it once you've arrived. Others will enjoy the comforts of camping in a familiar local spot, happy to be back in their favorite place. Although there are fewer things to worry about when organizing a trip closer to home, planning is still crucial so that everything goes as smoothly as possible. Whether you want to go large or low-key, think about the following factors before you go ahead and book your stay:

∼ WHO WILL ∼ YOU GO WITH?

A once-in-a-lifetime camping trip is probably best done in small numbers or alone (if you're brave enough), but if you're planning to go with a large group of friends or family then a basic camping trip for a short duration may be more manageable.

Traveling in a group means more differing opinions, which often leads to more arguments and a divide in the pack. Some will be more outspoken than others and you may end up not having much of a choice. Organizing things for lots of people can be a bit of a headache and there's the possibility of certain people not being able to pay straight away or even dropping out. These issues can arise when organizing any type of trip, but can be more problematic when camping because, as you will be largely self-sufficient, there's a lot more to think about.

A best friend or partner you can rely on and trust, who you know won't start an argument over trivial matters, will be your best option when buddying up, but always think wisely before you ask them if they'd like to join you—you will be living in close quarters with them while you're away.

Of course, if you have a family, the likelihood is that you'll want to go with them. Camping with children has many benefits: they can roam free in the fresh air (something that is happening less frequently these days) while you get some peace and quiet, and they can start to learn practical and essential skills.

CAMPING ALONE

If you think you could do it alone (and if you want to, of course!), *always* give two friends or relatives a realistic itinerary (your locations and dates) and keep a copy for yourself at all times. It might be best to laminate the document so that it won't get ruined in the rain. Alternatively, there are apps you can download on your phone and GPS devices that track your whereabouts and offer information on your closest detected location. If you're visiting a national park and there are rangers patrolling the grounds, give them your itinerary and contact number, and get theirs, in case of an emergency.

Always keep a phone on you—even if you don't have reception you may still be able to ring the emergency service numbers. Agree in advance convenient times to call a friend or family—then stick to these times so that they don't worry about your safety.

Make sure you're in a physically fit and healthy condition in advance of your trip. Book a doctor's appointment before you go if you're experiencing anything that's out of the norm.

Read up on survival skills and practice important camping drills in preparation. Campfire building, navigation, weather forecasting, and first-aid are all important things to know. It's also best to try a night under the stars in your yard (or a friend's) as a dress rehearsal to squash any fears before the big event.

Keep busy with planned excursions and activities, as it can be easy to worry and to start feeling lonely if you don't have anything organized. Plan these prior to the trip to help you make the most out of your camping experience.

I FELT MY LUNGS INFLATE
WITH THE ONRUSH OF SCENERY
—*air, mountains, trees,*
PEOPLE. I THOUGHT,
"THIS IS WHAT IT
IS TO BE HAPPY."

★ *Sylvia Plath* ★

≈ DECIDING WHERE ≈ AND WHEN TO GO

If you have decided to go alone then the only opinion you have to worry about is your own. If you're camping with other people, it's best to chat with them first about their preferences before you set your heart on a destination. If your idea of a fun time is very different to the person or people you've agreed to go with, perhaps now is the time to reconsider your fellow camper(s) or decide if you're willing to compromise. Giving their ideas a chance might lead you to partake in something you really enjoy but weren't open to before. If they love the beach and you love mountainous landscapes, you could always arrange to experience both by planning a road trip.

It might sound obvious, but if you've chosen a cold country it's best to go in its warmer months. Camping in T-shirt weather is much more favorable—not only will your luggage be lighter but there's a better chance of enjoying outdoors activities without getting chilly. Also check the average rainfall for the season you'd like to go in, as often you'll find that the months in between the peak summer and winter periods are quite damp and gray—and there's nothing worse than wearing soggy socks. Finally, if it's an option, consider going while school is in session, as campground prices increase dramatically during school holidays.

≈ BUDGET ≈

One of the biggest benefits of basic camping is how cheap it is compared with staying in more formal accommodations. If you don't like the idea of roughing it, renting an RV or glamping will cost significantly more, but they're still cheaper than staying in a hotel. When working out your camping budget, you need to factor in the following expenses: transport, campground fees, equipment, food and drink, days out, and a small buffer for any unexpected costs.

★ **Camping gear**—if you aren't already set up with a tent and sleeping bag, etc., you'll need to factor equipment into your budget. See "Equipment and gear," page 33, for more information on what you need to take with you.

★ **Transport**—if you're planning to go camping on the other side of the world, expect to pay up. You'll need to think about the costs to/from the airport or ferry port and to/from the place you're staying. Renting a car will cost extra per day, plus you'll have to pay for the fuel. Of course, if you're going local, then you'll probably only need to pay for fuel or your public transport ticket. Think of every possible travel expense, so that parting with your money isn't a surprise when you get there.

★ **Campground fees**—these vary depending on where you want to stay and what you're staying in. Sleeping in a tent will be cheaper than staying in a camper, while choosing a spot that has electricity or Wi-Fi may be an additional extra. Popular locations that have a good view and are well connected are more expensive due to their attractiveness and convenience. You can save a lot of money by staying somewhere remote—or, if you have a very tight budget and your chosen destination allows it, why not try out wild camping (see page 11)?

★ **Food and drink**—bringing along your own food and drink to a campground is strongly encouraged. Not only will you experience true camping, but you'll make huge savings. If you do forget to stock up on food before you arrive, make the extra journey to the nearest supermarket rather than buying your essentials at the local campground store (if they even have one), where they're bound to be more expensive. Think about the available cooking facilities before you go straight to the chilled aisles—if you don't have a fridge, it's best to avoid items that can spoil quickly (such as meat and dairy products); if you don't have a stove, then anything that needs to be heated up will be useless to you. Non-perishable foods (see page 79) will last the longest and are unlikely to get damaged in transit.

★ **Days out**—of course, some activities are free, such as walking and swimming in the sea, but you may want to visit the local village and buy some souvenirs, or try out that water sport you've been itching to do for a long time. This is your vacation, after all, so keep some money aside to make it extra special.

★ **Unexpected costs**—it's difficult to predict what life will throw at us, but it's always best to factor in a little extra money for emergencies. For example, you might need to buy medication for a sick member of your group, or you may forget an essential piece of clothing or equipment that has to be replaced quickly. While some unexpected purchases can't be avoided, you can protect your bank balance to some extent with travel insurance and up-to-date breakdown coverage if you're traveling by car or camper.

The stars were better
COMPANY ANYWAY.
They were very beautiful,
AND THEY ALMOST
NEVER SNORED.

★ *David Eddings* ★

EQUIPMENT AND GEAR

∼ CHOOSING THE ∼ RIGHT TYPE OF TENT

There are many factors you should consider when looking to buy a tent for your camping trip. For example, how many people does it need to sleep? What shape would you prefer it to be? What will the weather conditions and environment of your campground be like?

First, let's have a look at some of the most popular tent styles that are on the market:

 **The basic ridge tent**—this comprises poles at either end of the tent, as well as a pole that holds up the ceiling. Ridge tents are stable and easy to erect, and come in all different sizes. However, they can be too small for those who are taller than hobbit height, and are generally only practical for sleeping in.

 **Dome tent**—these tents have two very flexible poles that cross at the highest point of the tent's structure and make it dome-shaped. They're a lot taller than ridge tents due to the more vertically angled sides; however, they aren't as stable, especially if you're looking to go large and accommodate the whole family or a group of friends.

Geodesic and semi-geodesic tents—if you see a tent that is structured by a number of poles criss-crossing at different heights, it's geodesic. Its complicated shape gives it stability, so it's usually the recommended option for camping trips where you'll be exposed to the elements or sleeping on rough terrain. Semi-geodesic tents are similar but have a simpler structure.

 **Pop-up or quick-pitch tents**— these tents are designed to take any stress or challenge out of pitching up. Most are fitted with a sprung frame, meaning they quite literally pop open to a tent-like form. These are particularly useful if you have children who are constantly on the go and time is of the essence. They come in all shapes and sizes, but should only be used in less extreme surroundings. Make sure you know how to fold away your pop-up tent before you head off, as some can be quite tricky to flatten.

THIS IS THE POETRY, THE JOY OF A WILD *and roving existence,* **WHICH CANNOT COME TOO OFTEN.**

★ *Josiah Edward Spurr* ★
on camping

∼ CHOOSING THE ∼ RIGHT SIZE TENT

Tents are measured in berths, which refers to the number of people and amount of luggage they can hold. When browsing for their humble camping abode, lots of people make the mistake of choosing a berth size just big enough for the number of people who will be using the tent but often forget that each person will be carrying at least one backpack—not to mention extra bags, coolers, and other camping equipment.

If you'll be sleeping in a tent with one other person, it's usually recommended that you buy a tent with a berth of four; if there are three of you, then a five-berth tent is advisable. However, if you know that your luggage amounts to a week's worth of clothing and the kitchen sink, then it's a safe bet to choose the next berth up from what's recommended. You don't want to end up having to decide whether it's you or the luggage that sleeps outside.

≈ HOW TO PROLONG ≈ YOUR TENT'S LIFE

Purchasing a tent and all the extras for your big camping trip can burn quite a hole in your pocket, so follow these tips to help make your tent last longer:

★ Purchase a groundsheet protector or create a makeshift one (see page 64), as the groundsheet is the part of the tent most likely to suffer from wear and tear.

★ Always be careful when feeding the poles through the tent's material so you don't rip the fabric. Rub a layer of lubricant onto the poles before you erect the tent to make it easier to slide them through. Regularly apply lubricant on the tent's zips to stop them from jamming and eventually breaking.

★ While your tent is pitched, regularly check that stones or any other sharp objects haven't entered it, as these could rip the groundsheet.

★ If camping in direct sunlight, cover your tent with a sheet or tarp to help protect it from UV exposure.

★ Every time you use your tent, remember to wash the fabric and poles down with soapy water when you're back at home, then let it dry before you pack it away—especially if you've camped near the sea— to prevent corrosion.

★ If you don't use your tent frequently, clean and reproof the fabric every so often with the correct products, and never machine wash or tumble dry it.

∽ CHOOSING THE ∽ RIGHT SLEEPING BAG

If you want to purchase a sleeping bag for your camping trip, always take into account how chilly it will be at night in the place where you're staying and how susceptible you are to the cold. It's best to take your time looking at your options before rushing into buying the first one you see, as it's one of the most important pieces of gear you'll need when out under the stars.

Sleeping bags come in different shapes: the most common are mummy sleeping bags (those that look coffin-like) and rectangular sleeping bags, both of which are also available for children. Those who like to wrap themselves up in their duvet at night would probably lean towards the mummy style as the enclosed space keeps the heat in, although movement is slightly restricted. The more traditional, rectangular-shaped bags are for those who like to shuffle from side to side while asleep. Some rectangular sleeping bags can be doubled up if you want to share your space with your partner; check on the label if this function is available.

You should find at least one of three ratings on the labels of most sleeping bags. Comfort ratings signify the warmth of the sleeping bag— if you get hot quickly, it's better to go for a low rating, and if you get cold quickly, choose a high rating. Extreme ratings are only required if you plan to camp in freezing conditions, while season ratings are displayed to help you decide on the most suitable sleeping bag for the time of year you're camping. The most convenient rating to refer to is the season rating, which ranges from one to five—one being ideal for hot countries or camping in the peak of summer, and five being suitable for the harshest, most wintery conditions.

Take into account the weight and bulk of the sleeping bag. If you're planning on using your RV or car as a luggage vessel, this won't be something you need to worry about, but if you want to be able to hike from one place to the next with your sleeping bag strapped to your back then it needs to be lightweight without sacrificing quality and warmth.

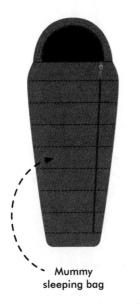

Mummy
sleeping bag

Rectangular
sleeping bag

WHATEVER FORM IT TAKES, **CAMPING IS EARTHY,** SOUL-ENRICHING *and character-building.*

★ *Pippa Middleton* ★

≈ CHOOSING THE ≈ RIGHT BACKPACK

There are several factors you need to consider before you purchase a backpack for your camping trip. It will be one of the key items you take with you, especially if you're hiking from site to site, and if you buy the wrong one, you may end up falling out with it.

★ **Don't impulse buy**—everyone loves a sale, but just because a backpack is 70 percent off, that doesn't mean you should buy it without browsing first. There are discounts and offers on throughout the year, so bide your time until you find something suitable for you. Don't be seduced by a backpack's attractiveness or color either.

★ **Quality**—don't look at your backpack as just a bag, but see it as the keeper of all your belongings for the duration of your camping trip. It needs to be comfortable, durable, and fit well. If you want to check all these boxes, expect to pay more than you might anticipate—but you'll be thankful for purchasing a good quality product once you're on the road. While you don't have to buy a super expensive backpack, make sure it's at least middle of the range, as the cheaper you go, the less comfortable it'll be.

★ **Size**—backpacks are measured in liters, which might seem strange if you've never had a backpack before. The best advice is not to concentrate on how many liters it holds but to use common sense and check to see if it's big enough to hold the amount of clothes you'd like to take. (We'll talk about packing later in this chapter.) Also, remember that you may be carrying your backpack a lot. Purchasing the biggest of them all will put a massive strain on your body, especially if you're small in height and frame.

★ **Padding**—the more cushioning on the shoulder straps and hip belt, the better, as this will help alleviate some of the stress being put on your body.

★ **Extra rucksack**—a lot of backpacks come with an extra daypack that you can attach to the back of the backpack. These are really handy for all the day trips and excursions you'll have planned during your camping trip. However, when you're carrying all your luggage, make sure the rucksack isn't actually attached to the backpack itself, as this will cause great strain on your back. Instead, wear the rucksack on your front to even out the weight slightly.

TOP TIP

Never buy your backpack straight from the internet without seeing it. You should try it on and rummage through all the different compartments first—buying it online, without having vetted it in-store, stops you from doing this. Go to a store, wear it, and even take some clothes and shoes with you to see how they fit inside it. Don't worry that everyone is going to look at you like you're raving mad; this is a more common practice than you may think and the best way to tell if it's the right backpack for *you*.

WITHOUT THE INTENSE **TOUCH OF NATURE,** *you can never fully* FRESHEN YOURSELF!

★ *Mehmet Murat İldan* ★

≈ WHAT YOU ≈ WILL NEED

It's so easy to forget to pack something when you go camping—not only do you have to think about your everyday items, but you also have to consider the not so obvious, especially if this is your first time literally out in the sticks. To offer a helping hand, the following pages include checklists of items you'll need for short and long breaks away. (If you're wild camping, be frugal with what you pack.)

Basic items:

★ Tent

★ Spare tent pegs

★ Groundsheet

★ Mallet/hammer—to knock tent pegs into the ground

BEFORE YOU GO

★ Swiss army knife

★ Duct tape—useful for almost any emergency

★ Backpack and daypack

★ Sleeping bag—double up two sleeping bags if you're going somewhere cold

★ Pillow—save space by taking a blow-up pillow or a sweater

★ Waterproof jacket

★ Cell phone and charger

★ Map

★ Guidebook

★ Ear plugs—if it's your first time camping, you might find that your senses are overactive

★ Flashlight/headlamp—plus spare batteries

★ Trash bags—picking up all your trash is the number-one camping rule

★ String/cord—to use as a makeshift washing line

★ Food and drink

★ Lightweight stove/grill

THE CAMPER'S SURVIVAL GUIDE

★ Gas/charcoal—remember to take a fire starter if using charcoal

★ Matches/lighter

★ Saucepan(s)

★ Bowl(s)/plate(s)

★ Cutlery

★ Water bottle

★ Water filter or treatment tablets

★ Bowl for doing dishes and dish detergent

★ Washcloth and dishcloth

★ First-aid kit—see page 62 for a checklist of medical items

★ Biodegradable soap

★ Wet wipes

★ Toilet paper

★ Travel towel—made of a material that takes up less than half the room of a normal towel

★ Toothbrush and toothpaste

★ Sunscreen

If you're traveling with a camper or a car, then you'll be able to take more with you and most of the items in the extras list will be appropriate to you. If you're planning to travel by public transport or on foot, then you'll be limited and should stick to the basics list.

Extra items:

- ★ Driver's license(s)

- ★ Sleeping mat/air mattress—for a comfier night's sleep (don't forget the pump if taking an air mattress)

- ★ Tarp/sun shade

- ★ Windbreak—for privacy

- ★ Foldable chairs and table

- ★ Electrical extension cord—to power low-wattage electrical appliances

- ★ Kettle or stovetop coffee pot

- ★ Lantern

- ★ Kitchen utensils

- ★ Cooler/freezer bag

THE CAMPER'S SURVIVAL GUIDE

★ Can opener

★ Hand mirror

★ Insect repellent

★ Bike(s)

★ Bike rack—if traveling by car or RV

★ Hiking poles

★ Umbrella

★ Games and books

★ Camera

★ Binoculars

★ Star chart

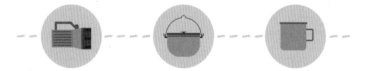

AT SOME POINT IN LIFE
THE WORLD'S BEAUTY
BECOMES ENOUGH.

★ *Toni Morrison* ★

CLOTHES—DRESSING ∼ APPROPRIATELY ∼

What clothes you take with you will depend entirely on where you're going and when. For example, you won't need your swimwear if you're planning to visit Norway in midwinter! Nevertheless, it's sometimes tricky to decide what to pack when you have limited space, and the weather can be unpredictable if you're camping somewhere like the UK.

As a rule of thumb, you should avoid wearing black in the summer, as the color will absorb the heat and leave you feeling like a radiator. On the other hand, white reflects the heat. If you're camping somewhere hot and you don't like white, go for pale colors instead, as they'll have more or less the same effect. It's also best to wear natural or moisture-wicking fabrics (such as cotton, linen, or polyester) to help increase the airflow to your skin, while loose-fitting or floaty outfits will help your skin stay cooler. If you are hiking, choose clothes made of synthetic material, as fabrics such as cotton and linen trap moisture.

A baseball cap is useful for blocking the sun from your eyes and will keep your face protected from the UV rays. Alternatively, a mid-brimmed or floppy hat will do the job, although some may find a floppy hat too distracting when embarking on a long trek. A more practical option to protect your face from the sun is a headscarf or buff, especially if you need to create more luggage space.

One material to avoid while camping during the summer months is denim. Even if you wear your trusty jeans every day of the week and can't bear the thought of leaving them behind, take heed, as they come with many disadvantages. Firstly, denim traps heat and will make you feel hotter than you are. Secondly, jeans take up essential space. Lastly, if you're wearing jeans out in the rain you should be prepared to have a soggy bottom and heavy legs for the rest of the day—denim takes a long time to dry out, especially if the sun isn't shining.

If you're going camping in the winter or somewhere cold, bring double or triple of all your items of clothing. Always take one or two layers more than you think you'll need to abate any fears about being chilly. Unlike the fabrics you'd wear in the summer, you'll need to stock up on items made of merino wool and insulating synthetics.

For cold-weather or winter camping, your base layers should be tight-fitting to your skin to trap heat, and moisture-wicking to prevent the absorption and retention of moisture. Your middle layers should be made of either wool or fleece, and buy sweaters or hoodies where the neck is longer than usual to keep the drafts out. For your top layers, you need a coat or jacket that will provide warmth and act as a barrier against the rain and wind. If you've chosen your other layers well and you're sure that you won't be facing extremely cold conditions, you might want to wear a lightweight jacket to allow more movement.

To protect your legs from the cold, take the same measures as for dressing your top half. Wear moisture-wicking leggings (the ones you wear to do exercise) or thermals for your base layer, and waterproof pants (thick or thin depending on how cold it'll be) for your top layer.

Lastly, a lot of heat escapes from the extremities of your body, so don't forget your hat, gloves, scarf/neck warmer, and big, woolly socks—and try to keep these dry, as they're less effective when wet.

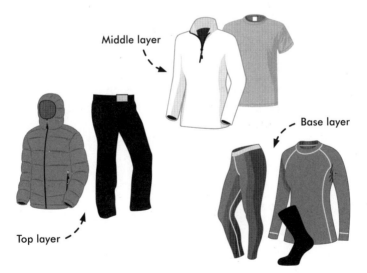

Middle layer

Base layer

Top layer

TOP TIP

If you're traveling with someone, don't take double of what you need. For example, if you both use a hairbrush and don't mind sharing, then just take one, or share your sunscreen and toothpaste—this means you'll have less to carry and you'll be able to fit extra items in your bag.

THERE'S A SUNRISE AND *a sunset every single* DAY, AND THEY'RE ABSOLUTELY FREE. *Don't miss so many of them.*

★ *Jo Walton* ★

≈ FIRST-AID KIT— ≈
WHAT YOU NEED

When you're alone or with very few people, you need to be more prepared for an emergency than usual—and you need the proper equipment in order to carry out first-aid. Here's a list of the main items you should pack in your bag of medical goodies:

★ Prescription medicine—if required

★ Painkillers

★ An assortment of strong fabric band-aids—water-proof band-aids will slip off the minute you start to sweat

★ Blister pads

★ Gauze bandages

★ Safety pins

★ Antiseptic wipes and cream

★ Antiseptic gloves

★ Eye wash

★ Burn gel/cream

★ Sunscreen

★ Sunburn relief (Aloe Vera gel)

★ Insect repellent

★ Cream for relief from insect bites and stings

TOP TIP

It's a nightmare when you're trying to get some sleep and all you can feel is the lumps and bumps of the ground beneath you. Try this hack for a comfier time camping.

Buy some interlocking foam floor tiles (the ones that are used in children's nurseries) or a couple of yoga mats. Once you've pitched your tent, put these down on the base of the tent for extra padding. Happy comfy camping!

CHOOSING YOUR TRANSPORT

If you want to experience complete peace and quiet, you have a greater chance of achieving this by wild camping in the middle of nowhere. However, taking a car or camper on your camping trip will give you access to more places and throw up fewer issues than camping with only a tent. Whether you want to hire or buy a camper, the list below gives details of the different ones on the market and their benefits:

★ **Twin-axle campers**—these vehicles are usually big and heavy and therefore require twin axles. This makes them easier to tow but difficult to park.

★ **Teardrop trailers**—these are compact and easy to tow. Due to their size, there isn't much floor space—most are just big enough to allow for a double bed.

★ **Pop-top campers**—the roofs of these campers can extend upwards when stationary, creating extra headroom.

★ **Folding campers**—these look like your average trailer when towed, but once erected they transform into fully fledged campers. Although their set-up is quite time-consuming, they can be neatly stored when not in use and they're easy to manoeuvre.

★ **Airstream campers**—if you can afford camping in style and luxury, these silver bullets are a must-have. However, they will set you back almost $100,000— well, we can all dream…

If you don't want to tow a camper, RVs are a fantastic alternative, especially to rent. RVs range in size and quality, and can come with a fixed roof, high-top, or rising roof, or over-cab beds.

THE EARTH HAS
music for those
WHO LISTEN.

★ *George Santayana* ★

DRIVING LAWS AND REGULATIONS FOR TOWING CAMPERS OR RVS

According to the United States Department of Transportation, different states and municipalities have different requirement based on the size and weight of what you are towing, especially if it is over eight feet wide. Some states may require special permits and licenses, or additional equipment such as side and rear-view mirrors. Your local motor vehicle administration will have the requirements and rules that will affect your travel. If you plan to travel through other states, don't forget to check their requirements as well.

When you're driving an RV, the laws also differ from state to state. If you're driving a motorcoach, where people can freely walk around while the RV is in motion, you may want to check on the relevant seatbelt laws. In addition, open container laws may apply to you if you are carrying alcohol in your fridge. It's technically allowed in many states, since an RV is considered a domicile, but make sure it's not within the driver's reach—you don't want to get pulled over and be faced with a questioning police officer! There may also be rules for transporting propane or other gases or fuels through tunnels.

Another issue that could come up is the transportation of firearms. Rules for how, when, and where you carry a firearm vary from state to state, so make sure to look up the rules for transporting and carrying firearms in each state you plan on traveling through. Lastly, don't forget to contact your insurance company to make sure you have the proper coverage!

≈ DRIVING ≈ AN RV

The last thing you want to happen when you take your RV on its first (or second, third, or fourth...) adventure is to total it or have part of it repaired. Follow these tips to ensure you drive your rental or own camper as well as possible:

★ Create a checklist of things that need to be secured down, locked, or tidied away before you set off driving—you don't want plates flying onto the floor and smashing just because you forgot to put them away. Also, if doors aren't shut properly, they could swing open when you turn the vehicle and cause damage to other furniture.

BEFORE YOU GO

★ Know the size of your RV—there are many road signs warning of height and width restrictions. Instead of disregarding them, as plenty of car owners do, make sure you take note, as you could damage your RV otherwise. Before setting off, write down the dimensions of the vehicle—you can find them out by looking online (take into account any added extras, such as a bike rack or roof box) or measuring it yourself—and display the measurements so they're easy to see when you're driving. Jot down the numbers in both feet and meters so you don't get caught out in a foreign country.

★ Keep the manual on you at all times—this will have all the key information you need if you encounter a problem with your RV. Also jot down the details of some local mechanics in the area you're visiting, and always ensure you have insurance and breakdown coverage for your trips.

★ Check in advance for toll booths—search your route online before you go to see if you'll need to have some money handy for toll charges. Remember that RVs will probably cost more than cars.

★ Plan ahead for gasoline and take a spare can with you. It's worth having a spare tire or plug kit, too.

★ Drive safely—RVs drive very differently from cars, plus they're more than double the size and weight. They're slower, take longer to come to a stop, and are more difficult to handle. Don't drive it as if it were a small hatchback—instead take your time and check your mirrors twice as often as you would driving a car, especially when turning and changing lanes. Additionally, take extra care overtaking other vehicles, as it'll take longer to accelerate past them.

★ Lock up when leaving your RV unattended—although your RV park may feel safe, you never know when thieves are lurking, so always be cautious about leaving your vehicle unlocked when you aren't there, even if you're just dashing to the campground's bathrooms. It's best to keep expensive items, such as electronic gadgets, out of sight.

THERE WAS NOWHERE
to go but everywhere,
SO JUST KEEP ON ROLLING
UNDER THE STARS.

★ *Jack Kerouac* ★

≈ RV ≈ MAINTENANCE

If you don't use your camper very often, ensuring that it's working properly before embarking on your trip is essential—you don't want your holiday to be put on hold while you wait for a towing service to come to the rescue. Follow these maintenance tips to make your journey smoother:

★ Service the RV regularly—although this may seem like an unnecessary expense, servicing your RV should extend its life, as essential fluids are replaced and the vehicle is given a once-over "health check."

★ Check the condition of your tires and make sure they have the required amount of air inside. If they look disfigured or if they're bald, replace them instantly.

★ Test all the electronics and replace any broken bulbs.

★ Check that the handbrake is easy to move up and down and hasn't seized up.

★ Test that all the kitchen appliances work.

★ Give your RV a good cleaning before and after your trip. Don't leave it in a mess when you get home as it'll only be twice as tricky to clean the next time you use it!

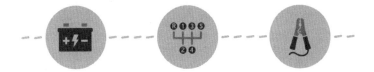

～ DRIVING A ～ RENTED VEHICLE

If you're planning to rent an RV or car, take into consideration the following things:

★ Take your driver's license and the licenses of any traveling companions who will take turns driving.

★ Research whether you'll need to apply for any international driver's permits and take these with you too.

★ Take an extra form of ID (such as a utility bill or passport) with you.

★ Remember to take the reservation details too.

★ Take your credit card—you'll need this for the rental and the deposit.

★ Check the pick-up time and location—if you arrive late, you could lose out on the vehicle as the company might offer it to someone else. If you're delayed, contact the number in the reservation confirmation to let them know.

★ Make sure you're given an inventory of all the items in the vehicle and check they are in fact there. If they aren't, make a note of this on the inventory, as well as of anything that is damaged, and hand the inventory back to the customer assistant. It's also worth taking dated photos of existing scratches, dents, and any damage you think they could hold you responsible for before you head off.

★ Always read the terms and conditions and the insurance policy extra carefully and query anything you don't understand. Some rental vehicles are only insured during the day and you must stop driving when the sun sets otherwise you'll be accountable for anything that happens after that time. Information like this is crucial to know, and you can find it all in the paperwork.

★ Ensure that the drop-off point is on your route— exploring your destination may mean that you want the start and finish points to be different. Double-check this information on the reservation confirmation as you could end up paying a fee if you return the vehicle to the wrong depot.

Between every two pines

THERE IS A DOOR

LEADING TO A

NEW WAY OF LIFE.

★ *John Muir* ★

CAMPGROUND MEALS

≈ STOCKING UP ≈ ON FOOD

Whether you're staying in a camper or tent, non-perishable food that can be eaten without fuss is what to look for when rummaging in the aisles of the supermarket. Here's a list of recommended foods to take for snacking and breakfasting on:

★ Granola bars or energy balls

★ Dried fruit

★ Fresh fruit—but only the hardy stuff, such as apples, pears, and oranges

★ Peanut butter or jam

THE CAMPER'S SURVIVAL GUIDE

★ Bread, rolls, or bagels—or all three

★ Crackers

★ Pre-made salads—including rice and potato salads to maintain your energy levels

★ Hummus and carrots

★ Cereal—if you like eating it dry

★ Nuts

★ Chips

★ Chocolate—remember to keep it cool, as sweaty chocolate is definitely not cool

★ Sugary sweets

★ Cold pizza—cooked the day before

★ The mighty Ramen

★ Granola bars

≈ CAMPING MEALS ≈

If you have a portable stove and gas or a grill, or your camper is kitted out with a stove top, you can have some fun cooking hot meals for your camping crew. Don't plan anything too fancy though, as you'll have limited space, appliances, and utensils. Also, if you don't have access to a fridge, the food items that you purchase and carry with you need to be non-perishable. Alternatively, you can go to the nearest store and buy your refrigerated goods just before you want to start cooking. Here's a list of favorite hot meals to have while camping:

THE CAMPER'S SURVIVAL GUIDE

★ Pasta

★ Scrambled eggs

★ Bacon

★ Nachos

★ Grilled ham and cheese

★ Salmon

★ Hot dogs and burgers

★ Toasted marshmallows—don't forget the sticks for holding them over your campfire

★ Roasted apples

If you're traveling with limited supplies and you're refrigerator-free, here's a list of handy key ingredients:

★ Fruit and veggies—such as corn on the cob, butternut squash, mushrooms, onions, apples, and oranges

★ Oatmeal

★ Pasta, rice, lentils, and beans

★ Canned tuna

★ Canned tomatoes

★ Cooking oil

★ Tea bags, instant coffee, and hot chocolate—if you have access to a kettle or campfire

★ Long-life milk

★ Water or fruit juice

TOP TIP

Those containers that small mints come in are the perfect size for storing salt, pepper, and spices—you'll never have a dull meal again, even if noodles are on the menu for the fourth day in a row. Just remember to eat all the mints first before pouring in your miscellaneous goodies!

COOKING AND EATING
food outdoors makes it
TASTE INFINITELY BETTER
than the same meal
PREPARED AND
CONSUMED INDOORS.

★ *Fennel Hudson* ★

WHILE YOU ARE AWAY

YOU'VE PLANNED YOUR CAMPING TRIP AND NOW YOU JUST NEED TO EXPERIENCE IT AND MAKE EVERY MOMENT COUNT! FROM PRACTICAL FIRST-AID ADVICE AND HANDY CAMPING HACKS TO IDEAS FOR KEEPING EVERYONE ENTERTAINED, THIS SECTION WILL BE YOUR GO-TO WHEN YOU GET ON THE ROAD.

CAMPING ETIQUETTE AND TIPS

≈ HOW TO FIND A ≈ GOOD PLACE TO MAKE CAMP

If you're wild camping and have the good fortune to be able to camp wherever you like, take heed of the following tips:

★ Never camp at the bottom of a hill or slope—it might feel sheltered there but if it rains, you'll soon know about it when your tent and all the ground around it becomes waterlogged. Instead, choose somewhere level which has slightly soft ground.

★ Make sure there are no hazards above you, such as power lines and trees, because if there are high winds, these could cost you your life.

★ Pitch your tent so that the back of it is facing into the wind for maximum protection from the elements.

★ Even if you love being near water, don't camp closer than 200 feet to the source—even further away is preferable. This is to ensure the preservation of the ecosystem it supports and is in line with wild camping's main rule of "leave no trace."

RAINSTORMS WILL TRAVEL THOUSANDS OF MILES, AGAINST PREVAILING *winds for the opportunity* **TO RAIN ON A TENT.**

★ *Dave Barry* ★

≈ CAMPGROUND RULES ≈

★ Don't be noisy. As you're out in the open, noise will carry further than usual, and you don't want to annoy your temporary neighbors. This is especially true at night, but try to keep it down in the day too.

★ Maintain a respectful distance from your campground neighbors. If possible, try to pitch up at least 20 feet away, although in the summer and busy periods this can become tricky. Don't let your table and chairs wander into their area, and make sure you use the paths of the campground rather than anyone else's area as a thoroughfare.

★ Leave your pitch area and other facilities as clean as you found them. It's your responsibility to dispose of any trash you've accumulated.

★ If camping with kids or dogs, make sure they're well-behaved and you know where they are at all times.

★ Don't ever drive in a campground to go short distances—for example, from your camping area to the toilets or campground store—as too many cars can be a hazard and cause noise pollution. Walk instead.

⌁ SPOT THE ⌁ DIFFERENCE

When everything looks the same it's very easy to get lost on a campground or in the countryside. If you're wild camping, try to choose a spot that is next to or near a memorable landmark. Perhaps there's a towering tree or a corner of a field that you'll remember easily. If you can't choose where you pitch up, this is where the following tip comes in handy.

To help you trace your tracks back to where you're staying, video yourself walking either to or from your tent to a place that's easy to spot. Focus on the landmarks you pass. If you're super-forgetful and don't mind getting strange looks, it might even be worth doing a running commentary while you're making the video to help prompt you.

∼ THERE'S A THIEF ∼ IN MY TENT

It's easy to get caught up in the friendly camping experience but always try to be safety savvy, as you wouldn't want your vacation ruined by thieves. Here are a few tips to help keep you protected at all times:

★ Although it seems like the logical thing to do, don't lock up your tent when you leave it. It'll only encourage thieves to think that you have valuables stored inside and a lock isn't going to stop them from tearing through the flimsy material of the tent.

★ There could be a very small possibility that thieves will try to steal things from your tent while you're sleeping. To beat them at their own game, the best place to stash your valuables is in the bottom of your sleeping bag. The thing that then lies between the thief and the valuables is you, sleeping soundly and holding the fort without even knowing it.

★ If the above does happen, and you wake up from slumber, do your best to restrain yourself from confronting or challenging an intruder. Instead, wait until they've left the area and then tell campground staff or the police. In the moment you may want to give them what they deserve, but it'll only provoke them more.

★ If you're going for a day trip and you're leaving your camper at the campground, remember to do a full check before you leave. Shut all the windows, lock all the doors, place all valuables out of sight (you shouldn't bring many expensive items with you for this reason in the first place), and fingers crossed, you won't have a problem.

There is something **INFINITELY HEALING IN THE REPEATED** *refrains of nature—* **THE ASSURANCE THAT** *dawn comes after night,* **AND SPRING AFTER WINTER.**

★ *Rachel Carson* ★

FIRST-AID ADVICE

Prepare yourself for any emergencies when you're out in the sticks by learning some basic first-aid skills. This is especially important if you're wild camping or there isn't a first-aid medic in your campground. The following techniques are the most commonly used in case of an emergency.

≈ WHAT TO DO IF ≈ SOMEONE IS UNRESPONSIVE BUT BREATHING

If a fellow camper is unconscious but still breathing, perform the following steps:

1. Open the airway by gently tilting the patient's forehead back with one hand and lifting the chin with the other.

2. Check for any signs of breathing—look out for chest movement, and sounds and heat coming from their mouth.

3. Put them in the recovery position (see page 100).

4. Call the emergency services for help and stay with the casualty, regularly checking if their breathing has changed at all, until they arrive.

∼ WHAT TO DO IF ∼ SOMEONE IS UNRESPONSIVE AND NOT BREATHING

If your fellow camper is unresponsive and not breathing, you will have to perform CPR (cardiopulmonary resuscitation), a combination of chest compressions and rescue breaths. But first, call the emergency services.

Chest compressions

1. Kneel beside the casualty and place the end of your palm towards the end of the breastbone in the center of their chest.

2. Place your other hand on top of the first and interlock your fingers but stay away from their ribs.

3. With your arms straight, lean over the casualty, pressing down on their breastbone by about 2 inches.

4. Keeping your hands where they are, release pressure until their chest is in the normal position—this is one compression. Repeat 30 times and keep in rhythm with the Bee Gees' song "Stayin' Alive" to help you keep the correct speed.

Rescue breaths (Note that the American Heart Association no longer recommends the use of "rescue breaths")
Once you've done a set of compressions, give the casualty two rescue breaths.

1. Open the casualty's airway, hold their nose closed, take a deep breath, and blow the air into the casualty's mouth until their chest rises.

2. Then lift away and let their chest fall. Repeat once more, followed by chest compressions, and continue until help arrives. If they start to breathe normally again, stop CPR and put them in the recovery position.

≈ HOW TO PUT ≈ SOMEONE IN THE RECOVERY POSITION

You will need to put someone in the recovery position if they become unresponsive.

1. Kneel down in front of the casualty and place their arm that's nearest to you at a right angle to their body, palm facing upwards.

2. Take their arm that's farthest from you and bend it so their hand is positioned on their opposite cheek, palm facing away from the cheek.

3. Lift their leg that's farthest from you so the knee is bent and the foot is flat on the floor. Next, roll them on their side by moving the bent knee across their body to the ground. As they roll over, the hand placed on their cheek should become a support for their head.

4. Gently tilt their head back to ensure their airway is open. Phone the emergency services and keep checking the casualty's breathing until they arrive.

~ HOW TO ~ APPLY A DRESSING

1. Firstly, wash the wound and make sure there's no dirt or grit in it.

2. For small cuts, just use a band-aid For anything bigger, use a sterile pad with bandage tape.

3. Cut the sterile pad so it covers the whole of the wound with a little extra to make sure there's space on all sides.

4. Place the pad on the wound, using surgical gloves if possible and making sure you don't touch the part of the pad which will be in direct contact with the wound.

5. Use ample amounts of bandage tape to hold the pad in place.

≈ SUNSCREEN, ≈ NOT SUN-SCREAM

You don't want to ruin your camping experience by getting sunburned—and sunstroke is no fun either, especially when you're sleeping in a hot tent. Even if you're good at applying sunscreen you can still get sunburned when you're outside all day. Here are some tips for staying safe in the sun that you might not have thought about before:

★ Don't apply sunscreen too thinly—although it's expensive and you want it to last as long as possible, you aren't going to be protected by putting on just a few blobs. Experts say that for each application, you should be using an ounce—enough to fill a shot glass—in order to cover your entire body.

★ To make applying sunscreen as easy a task as possible, use the spray-on kind. It's hassle-free and you won't have to put up with sticky hands for the rest of the day.

★ Remember to apply sunscreen to your neck and ears.

★ If you're going to wear sunscreen, wear it properly and make sure you reapply it—even if you've got the "all-day" stuff. It's easy to forget to do this when you're having such a good time, so it might be worth setting a time with your fellow campers for you all to reapply it.

★ Aim to stay in the shade for part of the peak of the day (between noon and 2 pm). This is tricky to do in reality but even staying in the shade for an hour will help decrease your chances of getting sunburnt or sunstroke.

★ Bring lip salve with you—you don't want your lips burning either!

≈ RECOGNIZING ≈ HEAT EXHAUSTION AND SUNSTROKE

Sunstroke or heatstroke is caused by the body overheating and being unable to bring down its core temperature to normal. It is usually preceded by heat exhaustion. Both can be prevented by staying hydrated, resting in the shade during the hottest part of the day, and limiting your exposure to the sun. Signs and symptoms of both conditions are as follows:

Heat exhaustion

★ Feeling tired and weak

★ Muscle aches

★ Feeling nauseous or being sick

★ Clammy skin

★ Heavy sweating

★ Headache

★ Diarrhea

★ Feeling confused, dizzy, lightheaded, or faint

★ Dark urine

Sunstroke

★ Hot skin to touch

★ Muscle cramps

★ Headache

★ Quick pulse

★ Core temperature 104°F or higher

★ Sluggish

★ Experiencing slurred speech, disorientation, agitation, hallucinations, or convulsions

★ Loss of consciousness

〜 TREATING HEAT 〜 EXHAUSTION AND SUNSTROKE

If you think the sufferer has heat exhaustion, make sure they have loosened or removed their clothes and sponge their body with cold water, or use wet towels. Keep them cool by fanning them and get them to drink something salty (a teaspoon of salt in a quart of water) to help replenish salt levels in their body and rehydrate them. If you think they have sunstroke, call an ambulance or take them to the nearest hospital immediately. While you are waiting, follow the steps above.

GAMES TO PLAY AROUND THE CAMPFIRE

In this section you'll find a variety of games to play, from using cards to pen and paper, ranging from those that are child-friendly to those that involve drinking.

⩗ CRAZY EIGHTS ⩗

Type of game:
Child-friendly

What you will need:
2–7 players
A deck of cards for 5 or fewer players; 2 decks of
    cards for more than 5 players

How to play:
Each player starts with eight cards, or seven if
there are only two players. Place the remaining
cards in a stack facedown in the middle of the
table. The top card is turned over, and play starts
as the player to the dealer's left discards a card
from their hand that is the same suit or same
number as the previous card that was dealt. Play
continues in this way, with the aim being to be
the first person to get rid of all their cards. If a
player can't go but they have a card bearing the

number eight, they can use this and announce a suit that the next player must put down. If the next player doesn't have any of these cards, they must pick one up from the face-down deck. Once a player has got rid of all their cards, the other players must add up their scores. Eights score 50, face cards score ten, and the other cards are scored at face value. These points are then passed to the winner. The overall winner is the person to score a total that is decided before the game—usually this is 100 points for two players, 150 points for three, 200 for four, 250 for five, 300 for six, and 350 for seven.

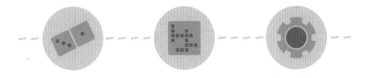

A PLAYFUL PATH
IS THE SHORTEST
road to happiness.

★ *Bernie DeKoven* ★

≈ G'DAY, BRUCE ≈

Type of game:
Child-friendly

What you will need:
A group of people (the more people, the better)

How to play:
Players sit in a circle and everyone starts with the name Bruce. Play follows like so:

Player one turns to their left and says "G'day, Bruce."

This player (player two) returns the hello with another "G'day, Bruce."

Player one then gestures to player three (the person to the left of player two) and says "Say g'day to Bruce, Bruce."

Player two turns to player three and the game begins again around the circle, with player two saying "G'day, Bruce."

If a player makes a mistake or if they hesitate for too long, their name changes and play starts again beginning with them. For the first mistake, their name changes to Sheila, then on their second mistake they become Harold, then Kylie, then Jason, then Lou, then Madge, and by the seventh mistake that player is out of the game.

For example, if player one makes a mistake then play would continue like so:

Player one turns to their left and says "G'day, Bruce."

Player two returns the hello with "G'day, Sheila."

Player one then gestures to player three and says "Say g'day to Bruce, Bruce."

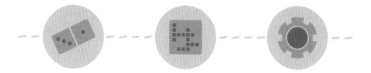

～ DOUSE! ～

Type of game:
Child-friendly

What you will need:
A group of players
Small cup
Water
Paper
Pen

How to play:
Players sit in a circle and someone is nominated to be the douser. The douser calls out a category, such as "cars," and writes down an example that they must not tell anyone else. The person to their left must think of an example in the category, such as "BMW," and say it aloud. As this is happening, the douser holds a small cup with water in it over the person's head. If they say

a different example from the douser's, then they are safe and play continues. If they say the same word the douser has written down, the douser must show their answer and tip the water over the player's head. That player then becomes the douser.

∼ MAU MAU ∼

Type of game:
Child-friendly

What you will need:
A deck of cards
2–6 players

How to play:
After choosing who goes first, players are dealt five cards each and the rest of the cards are placed face down in a stack. Play begins with the top card of the facedown deck being turned over and placed by the side of it, creating a discard pile. The aim of the game is to get rid of all your cards first, and players take it in turns, going counterclockwise, to place a card on the discard pile. This card must be either the same number or suit as the last card that was placed on the pile. If you can't go, you have to draw a card

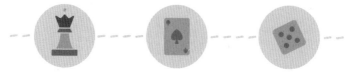

from the unused deck. Special cards change the play of the game, for example:

Jack—changes the suit. A jack can't be followed by another jack.

9—reverses the direction of play. For two players, play another card.

8—skips a turn.

7—the next player picks up two cards. If they're able to play a 7, the number of cards the following player has to pick up is doubled to four. If the following player also has a 7, then the next player must pick up eight cards.

Once you've discarded your second-to-last card, you must say "Mau." You must say "Mau Mau" before discarding your last card, otherwise you have to pick up a card.

∽ TRAVEL THE WORLD ∽

Type of game:
Drinking, but can also be played without alcohol

What you will need:
A group of people

How to play:
Players sit in a circle and someone calls out a country beginning with "T." The person to their left then calls out a country beginning with "R." Play continues and the aim of the game is to spell "travel the world" by saying countries' names that begin with the relevant letter. If someone hesitates, they must drink two sips (or they just lose, if playing the non-drinking version) and the game restarts with the person to their left. Country names cannot be repeated in a round.

≈ CAPS ≈

Type of game:
Drinking

What you will need:
2 players
Beer bottles
Beer bottle caps

How to play:
Two players sit apart from each other, each with a beer bottle and the bottle's cap placed upside down on top of it in front of them. Players take it in turns to knock the cap off their opponent's beer bottle by throwing spare bottle caps. (If you don't have any spare, it means you haven't drunk enough.) Fail, and it's the other player's turn; win, and the other player gets a chance to have another go at hitting your cap off. If they're not successful, they must down half of their drink. If they do win the challenge, then you must keep playing until someone fails.

SOMETIMES A FIRE BUILT ON A HILL

will bring interested people

TO YOUR CAMPFIRE.

★ *Shannon L. Alder* ★

NATURE'S WONDERS— WHAT TO LOOK OUT FOR

This short guide can be used for campers keen to spot some wildlife. Just remember that the animals you spot are wild—do not approach them!

≈ TRACKS AND SIGNS ≈

If you know what you're looking for, there are signs of wildlife everywhere—the soft mud near rivers and in woods is perfect for spotting animal tracks. Here are some things to watch out for while you're camping:

★ A paw print with five toes could be an otter or a badger. If there's a large pad behind the toe pads, it's probably a badger.

★ A paw print with four toes could belong to a fox or a dog. Look at the size of the rear pad—foxes have rear pads that are the same size as their toe pads, whereas a dog's rear pad is larger.

★ Deer tracks are easily identifiable by the two sausage-shaped slots made by their hooves.

Aside from tracks, look out for burrows near the water's edge, often with a patch of nibbled grass around the entrance, and piles of grass and stems with diagonal cuts at the end—these are all signs of water voles. Rats dig similar holes to water voles but they often have a heap of soil outside the entrance and the holes are connected by well-trampled paths. It's rare to see an otter, but you might see their droppings (or spraints)— these are approximately 3/4 to 2 1/2 inches long and contain fish bones and scales.

OUR TASK MUST BE TO
free ourselves from this
PRISON BY WIDENING OUR
circle of compassion to
EMBRACE ALL LIVING
creatures and the whole of
NATURE IN ITS BEAUTY.

★ *Albert Einstein* ★

CAMPING HACKS

Whether you're prone to tripping on your tent's ropes and are looking for a way to stop this or you're lost and need to find out quickly which way is north, this section contains the best camping cheats around.

≈ DUCT TAPE ≈ TO THE RESCUE

Arm yourself with a roll of duct tape. If you wake up in the morning to a collapsing tent, you can easily fix any broken poles by wrapping up the damaged parts with the strong stuff. It's also great for patching up practically anything, from holey backpacks or clothes to broken handles on saucepans and leaky water bottles.

≈ HYGIENIC HYDRATION ≈

Clean water is essential to life in any situation. If you're in a remote location and find yourself without it, you're in trouble. Presuming you can source water while you're camping, here's how to ensure it's drinkable.

The easiest way is to always carry water-purifying tablets—adding these to your H_2O will ensure it's safe. You can even stock up on water-purifying straws, which have the same effect. Boiling your water or using a water-purifying bottle are other ways to quench your thirst safely.

≈ DAYLIGHT MEASURE ≈

Imagine you're out walking—it's getting late and you're worried that you might not make it back to camp before dark. Put your mind at ease (or not) by estimating the amount of daylight left using nothing other than your bare hand.

Hold your arm parallel to the horizon with your fingers straight and your thumb tucked in. Line up your index finger with the bottom of the sun and count how many finger widths there are between the sun and the horizon. Each finger equals roughly 15 minutes of daylight. If there are 5 minutes of daylight left, start running!

Note: this only works if you are in the mid latitudes.

≈ FINDING NORTH ≈ AT NIGHT

If you're out in the wild and need to find your way without a compass, there's a simple method. (But let's just take a minute here to say that you should *never* embark on an unguided trip without a map and a compass!) Presuming you don't have any other options left, you can navigate by finding the North Star (Polaris)—as long as you're in the northern hemisphere.

First, you need to locate the Big Dipper, also known in the UK as the Plough, possibly the best-known constellation—if you don't know it already, you should definitely learn it. At the end of the Plough that's furthest from its "handle" you should be able to pick out the top-most star, on the top "lip" of the Big Dipper. From this point, extend your gaze in a straight line (away from the bottom of the Big Dipper) until you see a distinctly bright star. This is Polaris, your north point.

THOSE WHO CONTEMPLATE
the beauty of the earth
FIND RESERVES OF
STRENGTH THAT WILL
endure as long
AS LIFE LASTS.

★ *Rachel Carson* ★

≈ TICK ≈ REPELLENT SPRAY

Ticks can't hop, jump, fly, swim, or make noises—but they do have one hell of a grip when they bite, and once they have a hold on you they're nasty to remove. However, you won't even need to think about removing them when you use this tick-repellent hack to stop ticks coming near you in the first place.

Put one part tea tree oil and two parts water into a spray bottle. Spray the mixture on to your clothes, shoes, and tent to create a force field against the ticks.

≈ TAPE TRAIL ≈

Even seasoned hikers lose their way from time to time. If your travels have taken you into dense forest or woodland, finding your campground again can prove tricky, especially at night. You can take the stress out of the situation with this simple hack.

Invest in some brightly colored biodegradable tape, which you can use to mark out a key route through difficult environs. Leave small tabs in easy-to-spot places, or if you're really in the thick of it, and you're not going very far, run a longer stretch of tape out at waist height.

≈ BOTTLE BOOST ≈

Hydration is key when you're hiking. Investing in a sturdy, stainless steel water bottle is a great idea—they are less prone to cracking than plastic ones and contain no potentially harmful chemicals, and the double-skinned ones will maintain the temperature of the liquid inside for longer. Furthermore, you can give your bottle a boost and make it even better with this hack.

Wrapping your bottle in duct tape will increase its temperature-holding potential. In cold weather, it will also protect your fingers from a chill when holding the bottle. So it's a win-win!

≈ FOR-THE-WIN ≈ RAINBOOTS

If you've forgotten your rain boots and your only footwear consists of soft fabric that absorbs water far too quickly, you may feel like your camping holiday is doomed if the rain doesn't stay away. However, all is not lost with these makeshift wellies.

What you need:
4–6 plastic bags (without holes)
Duct tape
A small pair of scissors

How to make them:

1. With your shoes on, wrap a plastic bag around each foot and tie the handles firmly in a knot, though not so tight that you cut off your circulation.

2. With the scissors, in two more plastic bags, make holes that are big enough to slide your feet through. Put them around each leg so that they slightly overlap the other bags and tie the handles in a knot to secure them around your legs. Depending on how tall you are, you may have to repeat this step further up your calves.

3. Now here comes the duct tape—the more colorful and patterned it is, the better. Wind the duct tape round each leg, starting at your toes and finishing where the plastic bags meet your flesh or clothes. Remember to circle the duct tape two to three times where the two plastic bags meet and where the makeshift rain boot ends for extra waterproof protection.

4. Now you can do whatever you had planned without the weather stopping you.

THE STARS ARE LIKE THE TREES *in the forest,* ALIVE AND BREATHING.

★ *Haruki Murakami* ★

∽ STRIKE ME LUCKY ∽

Taking matches on a camping trip is pretty essential for all sorts of miscellaneous situations. However, the strike pads on "strike anywhere" matchboxes can be a bit temperamental. To ensure you don't have to do the rounds of your campground neighbors, asking if you can borrow their strike pads, also take a strip of sandpaper— or a nail file, if you want your luggage to be as multifunctional as possible!

⟩⟩ BOTTLE ILLUMINATOR ⟩⟩

Tired of holding a flashlight or your phone whenever you try to find something at night? Remember to pack a large water bottle and a headlamp with an elastic strap/headband. When it gets dark, secure the headlamp to the water bottle using its strap, so the light is facing inwards, and *voilà*—you have your very own free-standing lamp that illuminates the whole tent or area, not just wherever you're facing.

≈ TENT-ROPE ≈ IDENTIFIER

When it's dark, even if you're cleverly equipped with a flashlight, it's often difficult to see your tent—let alone the tent's ropes, which seem to be there for the sole reason of tripping you up.

This hack will help to reduce your chances of an accident, as well as enabling you to find that elusive tent entrance more easily. For each tent rope, take a swim noodle and cut it to the length of the rope—a brightly colored one will make your tent easier to identify. With a penknife, make a vertical slit down one side and into the middle of the swim noodle. Once you've pitched your tent, latch the foam pieces around the ropes. If you want extra visibility, decorate the pool noodles with glow-in-the-dark paint.

≈ EMERGENCY ≈ CRAYONS

A steady source of light is key when you're hiking or camping. You may need to shed light on various activities away from your campfire and in the absence of a flashlight (or one that has a working battery!) you can use this hack.

Wax crayons with paper casing are good for coloring and great for burning in a candle-like fashion when there are no other light sources to hand. You can get up to half an hour from a lit crayon. Just don't use your favorite color or your artwork will suffer!

⤳ GET BUSY ⤳ WITH BEESWAX

If you're keen on protecting the environment as well as staying dry while out walking, this one is for you. Waterproofing your gear is an essential precaution for any trek. However, most spray-on proofers are made up of various synthetic chemicals—if you'd prefer to avoid these, use this natural alternative.

Beeswax features in many proofing products, but used in its pure form, it does a similar job without having been heavily processed. It can be rubbed directly on to garments, bags, and shoes—just expect them to be a little waxy and pleasantly fragrant as a result.

～ DRY BOOTS ～

Whether your hiking boots are wet from working up a sweat or from trudging through huge puddles or a rainstorm, you'll want to let them dry as soon as you have the chance. Here's a hack to help you do just that.

Ball up some newspaper and stuff it (not too tightly!) into your wet boots. The paper will absorb the moisture and dry your boots out much quicker than heat alone would. If you've finished walking for the day, replace the paper after a couple of hours.

NATURE IS NOT
a place to visit.
IT IS HOME.

 ★ *Gary Snyder* ★

～ WASH AND GO! ～

If you're camping or on an extended walk and you've fallen in something brown and sticky (no, not a stick) but you're also miles away from a washing machine, you can use this hack.

Pack a large, durable ziplock bag. Stuff the soiled garment into the bag along with a small pinch or drop of laundry detergent, or some "pocket soap" (which you can buy from outdoor stores). Add water (hot or cold)—you might have to beg for water at a local residence if you don't have any to spare from your bottle. Mix everything well using your hands for 5 minutes, before sealing the bag and leaving to soak for 10 minutes. Then squeeze as much water out as possible before rinsing with clean water and squeezing again. Dry the garment on an elastic travel washing line or hang it up on a branch. If using this hack while hiking or outdoors, make sure you use 100 percent biodegradable soap.

∼ SUPERCHARGED ∼ SLEEPING BAG

If a cold night is in the cards, your sleeping bag needs to be up to the job. If you're concerned it might not be (or perhaps you can't afford a new one), consider this hack to boost your night-time comfort.

Those heat reflectors that sensible people put in their car windows to reflect the sun are naturally good at reflecting heat, so by slipping one (or two) into your sleeping bag, you'll create a layer of heat-reflecting insulation. You'll be as toasty as a turkey in tinfoil at 350°F.

≈ FIRE STARTER ≈

There's nothing better than having a BBQ with your friends or family on your first evening under the stars. But if there isn't an experienced fire starter among you, you could be starved of the sausages that are waiting to be cooked. Thankfully, that's where this hack comes in useful.

Instead of taking a big bag of charcoal with you, pack each piece of charcoal individually in the compartments of a 12 or 18-hole cardboard egg carton. Not only will this save you from lugging a heavy bag of charcoal round, but the egg box also acts as an easy-to-start fire pack. All you have to do is light the egg carton and the fire will catch on to the charcoal. Happy barbecuing, and make sure you roast some Starburst candies for dessert—delicious!

NATURE IS IMAGINATION ITSELF.

★ *William Blake* ★

HAPPY CAMPING!

Hopefully this little book has given you some insight into what to expect when you're camping and you'll be more prepared if you encounter any hiccups along the way. Embrace the peace and quiet of nature, and partake in plenty of outdoor activities to make your camping experience one you'll never forget.

Stay safe, be spontaneous and, most importantly of all, have fun!

If you're interested in finding out more about our books, find us at:

www.skyhorsepublishing.com

IMAGE CREDITS